BASEBALL

HISTORY
SOFTBALL
LEGENDS OF THE GAME

Amanda Bennett

This book belongs to

_____

Baseball:
History, Softball, Legends of the Game

ISBN 1-888306-00-9

Copyright © 1996 by Amanda Bennett

Published by:
Homeschool Press
229 S. Bridge St.
P.O. Box 254
Elkton, MD 21922-0254

Send requests for information to the above address.

Cover design by Mark Dinsmore.

Printed in the United States of America.

⚾ ⚾ ⚾

To Katie and Thad, our home grown sluggers,
with special thanks to my friend, Matt Ridpath,
for showing me that baseball
is a great way to enjoying learning!

⚾ ⚾ ⚾

How To Use This Guide

Welcome to the world of unit studies! They present a wonderful method of learning for all ages and it is a great pleasure to share this unit study with you. This guide has been developed and written to provide a basic framework for the study, along with plenty of ideas and resources to help round out the learning adventure. All the research is done. These are READY to go!

TO BEGIN: The <u>Outline</u> is the study "skeleton", providing an overall view of the subject and important subtopics. It can be your starting point—read through it and familiarize yourself with the content. It is great for charting your course over the next few weeks (or developing lesson plans). Please understand that you do not necessarily have to proceed through the outline in order. I personally focus on the areas that our children are interested in first—giving them "ownership" of the study. By beginning with their interest areas, it gives us the opportunity to further develop these interests while stretching into other areas of the outline as they increase their topic knowledge.

By working on a unit study for five or six weeks at a time, you can catch the children's attention and hold it for valuable learning. I try to wrap up each unit study in five or six weeks, whether or not we have "completed" the unit outline. The areas of the outline that we did not yet cover may be covered the next time we delve into the unit study topic (in a few months or perhaps next year). These guides are <u>non-consumable</u>—you can use them over and over again, covering new areas of interest as you review the previous things learned in the process.

The <u>Reading and Reference Lists</u> are lists of resources that feed right into various areas of the <u>Outline</u>. The books are listed with grade level recommendations and all the information that you need to locate them in the library or from your favorite book retailer. You can also order them through the national Inter-Library Loan System (I.L.L.)—check with the reference librarian at your local library.

There are several other components that also support the unit study.

The <u>Spelling and Vocabulary Lists</u> identify words that apply directly to the unit study, and are broken down into both Upper and Lower Levels for use with several ages.

The <u>Suggested Software, Games and Videos Lists</u> includes games, software and videos that make the learning fun, while reinforcing some of the basic concepts studied.

The **Activities and Field Trip Lists** include specific activity materials and field trip ideas that can be used with this unit to give some hands-on learning experience.

The **Internet Resources List** identifies sites that you might find helpful with this unit. The Internet is a wonderful resource to use with unit studies providing the sights and sounds of things that you might never otherwise experience! You can see works of art in the Louvre. See the sunrise on Mt. Rushmore, hear the sounds of the seashore and find many other things that will help provide an "immersion" in the unit study topic, as never before, without ever leaving home. As with any resource, use it with care and be there with the students as they go exploring new learning opportunities.

The author and the publisher care about you and your family. While not all of the materials recommended in this guide are written from a Christian perspective, they all have great educational value. Please use caution when using any materials. It's important to take the time to review books, games, and Internet sites before your children use them to make sure they meet your family's expectations.

As you can see, all of these sections have been included to help you build your unit study into a fun and fruitful learning adventure. Unit studies provide an excellent learning tool and give the students lifelong memories about the topic and the study.

Lots of phone numbers and addresses have been included to assist you in locating specific books and resources. To the best of our knowledge, all of these numbers were correct at the time of printing.

The left-hand pages of this book have been left "almost" blank for your notes, resources, ideas, children's artwork, or diagrams from this study or for ideas that you might like to pursue the next time you venture into this unit.

"Have fun &
Enjoy the Adventure!"

Table of Contents

Introduction

Baseball—just hearing the word can bring visions of exciting plays, great players, hot dogs, soda pop and peanuts in the stands and a great afternoon of fun. Many Americans get to play softball or baseball during their childhood as a neighborhood sport or as a member of a Little League team.

Some of us were never involved in the game and were unaware of the details or the history of the sport—and that includes the parents here at our house! Our children began to play on Little League teams and really got involved in baseball and softball, while my husband and I had no idea of the rules, the history or the strategy behind the game. In the meantime, this sport REALLY got their attention and they wanted to learn more about it in a unit study. As a result, we began an adventure that has been so much fun and very enlightening for ALL of our family.

This unit study has been developed to provide a complete look at baseball as a sport, using a cross-curriculum approach. Areas like geography, history, science and reading are included in this unique study, along with a lively introduction to math and sports statistics. Topics of the study include:

- History of baseball in America
- Rules and plays of baseball
- Players and legends
- Softball
- Science and math in baseball
- Baseball art and music
- Baseball collectibles

Enjoy the story of baseball and all that it holds in the way of a learning adventure! What better way to learn about forces and momentum than when studying why a curve ball curves, or learning about vibration by finding the sweet spot of a bat? Why is it important to warm up before playing a baseball game? Spend some time learning about reflexes and reaction time and the roles that they play in sports.

Use your imagination and spend some time off the bleachers—get into some great books and spend time out in the grass playing catch with your students to get in some "hands-on" learning and make some great memories. As always, enjoy the adventure and play ball!

Study Outline

I. History of baseball

A. Early beginnings—there were many games throughout history that were ball and stick types of games
1. Paddleball
2. Trap ball
3. Rounders
4. Town Hall
5. Cricket

B. Development of the game in the nineteenth century
1. It developed from a children's game into a game for all ages, and particularly held the interest of men
2. Baseball as we know it today first appeared in New York at the Knickerbocker Club, under the guidance of Alexander Cartwright (1845)
   a. Diamond-shape field
   b. Bases 90 feet apart
   c. Nine-man team
   d. Three outs for each of two teams in each inning
   e. First official game under Mr. Cartwright's rule was probably played on June 19, 1846
3. The first baseball league was formed in 1858, called the National Association of Base Ball Players
4. When the Civil War broke out, the game was spread to many sections of the country by Northern soldiers
5. The first professional team (salaried) was announced in 1869, the Cincinnati Red Stockings
6. The first professional baseball league, the National Association of Professional Base Ball Players, was formed by the players in 1871
7. In 1876, the National League was formed
8. Innovations for the game and the spectator were developed in the late 1800's
   a. The baseball glove was invented in the late 1870's
   b. Concessions were developed in the late 1800's to satisfy the growing crowd's hunger at games—these included hot dogs, soda pop and peanuts.

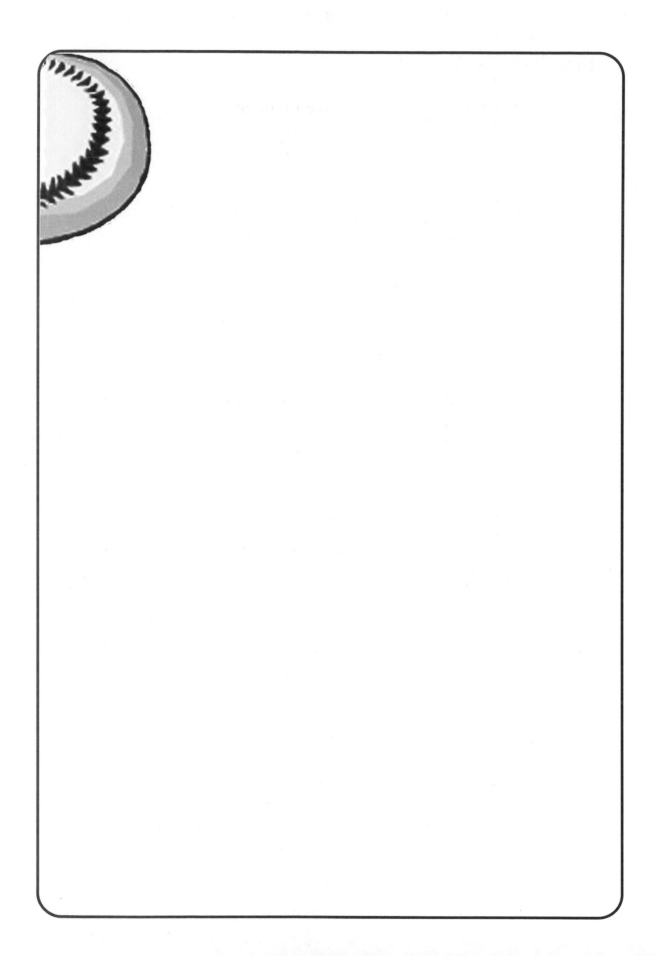

9. The rules were changed in 1884, permitting pitchers to throw overhand pitches
10. The American League was formed in 1899, and became a major league in 1901

C. Development of the game in the twentieth century
1. The National Commission for Baseball was formed in 1903 to oversee Major League Baseball
2. In 1908, the song "Take Me Out to the Ball Game" was introduced
3. Permanent baseball parks were built in the early 1900's baseball boom
4. Baseball grew rapidly in popularity in the early 1900's
5. The World Series began in 1903
6. World War I broke out, and many of the professional ball players joined the military
7. After the war, baseball's popularity came back
8. Andrew (Rube) Foster formed the Negro National League in 1920, in response to opposition to racial integration in the major leagues
9. In 1928, the Negro American League formed
10. Night baseball was begun in the major leagues in 1935
11. World War II brought hard times for major league baseball, as players joined the military and shortages in transportation and rubber slowed down the growth and interest in baseball
12. In 1943, Philip Wrigley started the All-American Girls Softball League
13. In the 1940's, black players were accepted into the major leagues
14. In the 1950's, franchises began to break away from their original hometowns to move to better towns and, hopefully, more income
15. As the games became televised, game times were scheduled later in the day, and baseball slowly became dependent on television

D. History of baseball leagues
1. Major Leagues
2. Minor Leagues
3. All-American Girls Professional Baseball League

4. Negro League
5. College League
6. Little League
7. Grapefruit League
8. Cactus League

II. Baseball—the game

A. The baseball parks
    1. Dimensions
        a. Infield is a square with 90 foot long sides
            (1) Pitcher's mound is an 18 foot circle
            (2) Pitcher's mound is 60.5 feet from home plate
        b. Outfield can be of varying dimensions
    2. Major League parks of yesterday and today
B. The team
    1. Number of players
    2. Positions
        a. Pitcher
            (1) Starting pitcher
            (2) Relief pitcher
        b. Catcher
        c. Infielder
            (1) First baseman
            (2) Second baseman
            (3) Third baseman
            (5) Shortstop
        d. Outfielder
            (1) Left fielder
            (2) Center fielder
            (3) Right fielder
    3. Batting order
    4. Designated hitter
    5. Regulars and reserves
    6. The staff
        a. Coaching staff
        b. Athletic trainers
        c. Team manager

C. The game play
1. A major league baseball game consists of nine innings
   a. An inning consists of each team staying at bat until they have three outs (each team has a half-inning)
   b. Extra innings can be played if the score is tied at the end of nine innings
2. The teams get set for play
   a. Home team is out in the field first
   b. Visiting team is first at bat
   c. Team managers choose players for each position, as well as a batting lineup
3. The pitch, the hit and the play
   a. The pitch
      (1) Strike—three strikes, player is out
      (2) Foul
      (3) Ball—four balls, player walks to first base
      (4) Hit by pitch—player advances to first base
      (5) Ball is hit into play
   b. The hit
      (1) Types of hits
         (a) Bunt
         (b) Ground ball
         (c) Line drive
         (d) Fly ball
         (e) Home run
      (2) Results of hits
         (a) Fly ball is caught—player is out
         (b) One-base hit is called a single
         (c) Two-base hit is called a double
         (d) Three-base hit is called a triple
         (e) Four-base hit is a home run
   c. The play—advancing around the bases
      (1) Running on a hit
      (2) Stealing bases
      (3) On a sacrifice
4. The umpires
   a. Enforce the game rules
   b. Call the pitches—strikes, fouls and fair balls
   c. Rule whether or not the runner is safe or out

III. Science in Baseball

A. Reflexes and reaction times—the roles they play in hitting and catching

B. Sliding into a base—using friction to help slow down to tag the base and stop

C. Making a ball curve or "break" with spin—using aerodynamics to help change the path of a ball

D. Leverage in baseball—the bat is a simple lever, and the load to be moved is the baseball

E. Gravity and the role it plays in bringing a thrown ball to the ground—why a thrown ball needs to have an arc to go longer distances

F. Rounding the bases to fight inertia—making the most of the runner's building speed while still tagging the bases using a curved path

G. Warming up before a game—providing muscles with extra oxygen to make them stronger and able to endure more than "cold" muscles

IV. The Major Leagues

A. The season of play
1. Spring training—to prepare for the upcoming season
2. Regular season play—162 games
3. Division playoffs for each league's pennant
4. Winners of the league pennants compete in the World Series

B. The American League (East and West Divisions)
1. Baltimore Orioles—Baltimore, Maryland
2. Boston Red Sox—Boston, Massachusetts
3. California Angels—Anaheim, California
4. Chicago White Sox—Chicago, Illinois
5. Cleveland Indians—Cleveland, Ohio
6. Detroit Tigers—Detroit, Michigan
7. Kansas City Royals—Kansas City, Missouri
8. Milwaukee Brewers—Milwaukee, Wisconsin
9. Minnesota Twins—Bloomington, Minnesota
10. New York Yankees—The Bronx, New York

11. Oakland Athletics—Oakland, California
12. Seattle Mariners—Seattle, Washington
13. Texas Rangers—Arlington, Texas
14. Toronto Blue Jays—Toronto, Ontario, Canada

C. The National League (East and West Divisions)
1. Atlanta Braves—Atlanta, Georgia
2. Chicago Cubs—Chicago, Illinois
3. Cincinnati Reds—Cincinnati, Ohio
4. Colorado Rockies—Denver, Colorado
5. Florida Marlins—Ft. Lauderdale/Miami, Florida
6. Houston Astros—Houston, Texas
7. Los Angeles Dodgers—Los Angeles, California
8. Montreal Expos—Montreal, Quebec, Canada
9. New York Mets—Flushing, New York
10. Philadelphia Phillies—Philadelphia, Pennsylvania
11. Pittsburgh Pirates—Pittsburgh, Pennsylvania
12. St. Louis Cardinals—St. Louis, Missouri
13. San Diego Padres—San Diego, California
14. San Francisco Giants—San Francisco, California

V. Famous players and the legends of the game (listed here are just a few of the people that come under this category)

A. Lou Gehrig
B. Dave Dravecky
C. Cy Young
D. Christy Mathewson
E. Frank Robinson
F. Jimmie Foxx
G. Babe Ruth
H. Tom Seaver
I. Billy Sunday
J. Brooks Robinson
K. Nolan Ryan
L. Mickey Mantle
M. Carl Yastrzemski
N. Dale Murphy
O. Dave Winfield
P. Dizzy Dean

Q. Roger Hornsby
R. Walter Johnson
S. Jackie Robinson
T. Jim Abbott
U. Rickey Henderson
V. Roy Campanella
W. Roberto Clemente
X. Willie Mays
Y. Willie Stargell
Z. Yogi Berra
AA. Hank Aaron
BB. Ted Williams
CC. Johnny Bench
DD. Ty Cobb
EE. Joe DiMaggio
FF. Whitey Ford
GG. Orel Hershiscr
HH. Reggie Jackson
II. Sandy Koufax
JJ. Don Mattingly
KK. Satchel Paige
LL. Cal Ripkin, Jr.

VI. Baseball Awards and Recognition

A. Most Valuable Player (MVP)
B. Rookie of the Year
C. Golden Glove
D. Cy Young Award
E. Manager of the Year
F. National Baseball Hall of Fame
G. League pennant
H. World Series winner

VII. Math in baseball

A. Batting average (BA)
B. Earned Run Average (ERA)
C. Slugging Average (SLG)

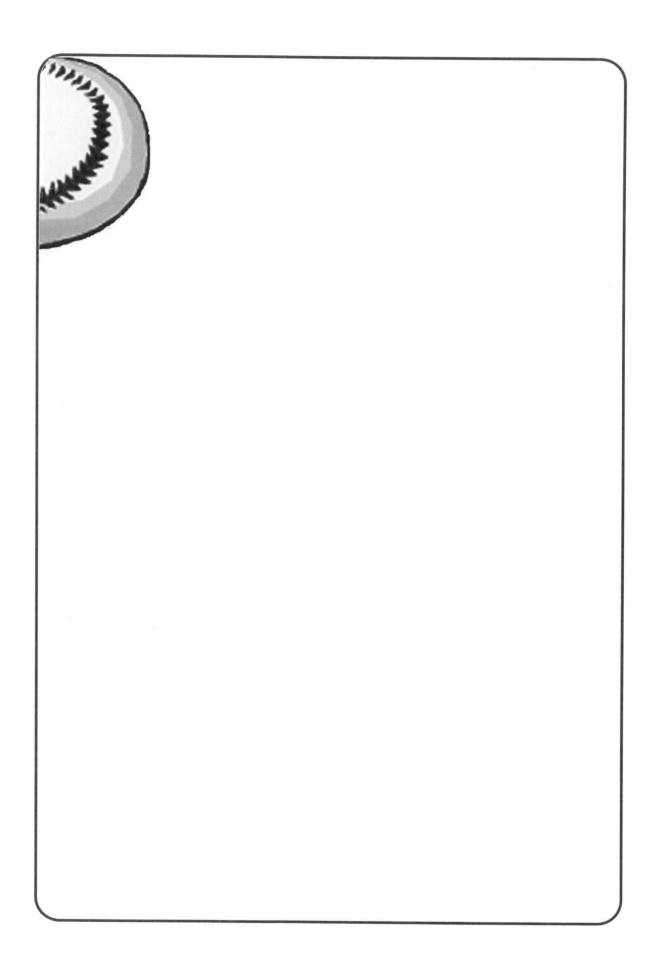

D.   On-base Average (OBA)

E.   Won-Lost Percentage

F.   Standings

G.   Runs Batted In (RBI)

VIII. Softball—the game

A.   It developed in Chicago in 1887 as a type of indoor baseball

B.   Popular with women and girls of all ages

C.   The games usually last seven innings

D.   Ball is pitched underhand
1.   Fast pitch
2.   Slow pitch

E.   The field
1.   Bases are 60 feet apart
2.   Pitcher's mound is 46 feet from home plate

F.   The National Softball Hall of Fame and Museum
1.   Oklahoma City, OK
2.   Inductees include legends like Joan Joyce and Herb Dudley

IX. Baseball and softball equipment

A.   Baseball

B.   Softball

C.   Bat

D.   Gloves

E.   Batting helmet

F.   Uniform

G.   Catcher's gear

H.   Cleats and shoes

X. Baseball collectibles

A.   Types of collectibles
1.   Baseball cards
2.   Baseball game ticket stubs
3.   Baseball player autographs
4.   Baseball art prints

5. Baseball posters
6. Baseball bats
7. Baseball caps
8. Baseball comic books
9. Baseball uniforms and shoes of players
10. Baseball team pennants
11. Letters from baseball players

B. Enjoying a baseball collection
1. Purchasing the items (baseball cards seem to be the most popular collectible)
2. Taking care of your collection
3. Pricing your collectibles
4. Keeping track of your collection, using handwritten lists or database software on the computer
5. Expanding your collection through trading and buying items from others

XI. Baseball art and music

A. Art—there are many works of art concerning baseball for you to enjoy in this baseball unit, and these are a few favorites
1. *Baseball Players Practicing* (1875), a watercolor painting by American master Thomas Eakins, on display at the Rhode Island School of Design
2. *Babe Ruth* (1984), a painted wooden sculpture by Armand LaMontagne, on display at the National Baseball Hall of Fame, Cooperstown, New York
3. *Baseball Game at Night* (1934), an oil painting by Morris Kantor, on display at the National Museum of American Art, Smithsonian Institution, Washington, DC
4. *July Fourth* (1951), an oil painting by Anna Mary Robertson Moses (Grandma Moses), on display at the White House, Washington, DC
5. *Game Called Because of Rain* (1949), an illustration for the cover of the Saturday Evening Post, by Norman Rockwell, on display at the National Baseball Hall of Fame and Museum, Cooperstown, New York
6. *The Dugout* (1948), an illustration for the cover of the Saturday Evening Post, by Norman Rockwell, on display at the Brooklyn Museum, Brooklyn, New York

B.   Music—there's plenty of music associated with a baseball game, and here are a few you can usually hear at a game
    1.   "Take Me Out to the Ball Game", lyrics by Jack Norworth and music by Albert von Tilzer
    2.   "The Star Spangled Banner" by Francis Scott Key

Spelling and Vocabulary
Lower Level

hit	baseball
bat	throw
ball	field
run	park
base	team
home	play
first	bench
second	out
third	foul
catch	swing
line-up	hat
batter	glove
runner	cleats
lead	shoes
single	uniform
double	name
triple	coach
fly	pants
steal	socks
pitch	shirt
visitor	card
hustle	collect
infield	number
outfield	buy
walk	cost
inning	sell
bleacher	save
chalk	clean
plate	name
fans	sort

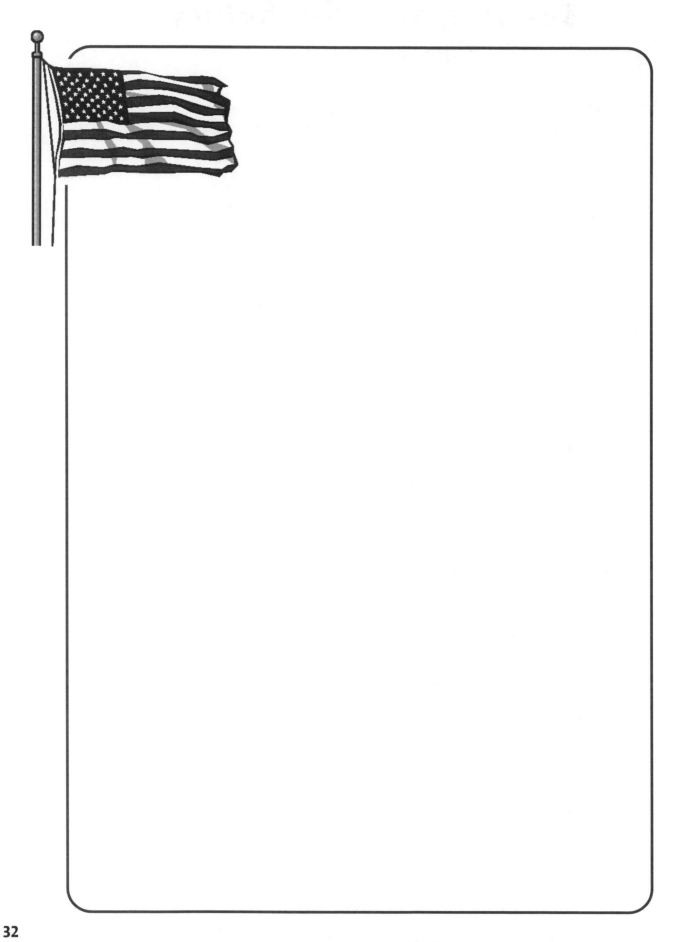

Spelling and Vocabulary
Upper Level

team
position
player
catcher
pitcher
infielder
outfielder
hitting
strength
coach

baseball
softball
rules
regulations
umpire
official
conduct
visiting team
home team
forfeit

inning
line-up
line drive
designated hitter
clean-up hitter
foul territory
sacrifice
shutout
forced out
intentional

agility
concentration
ability
aggressiveness
speed
quickness
velocity
leadership
dedication
teamwork

uniform
cleats
equipment
glove
favorite
batting helmet
batting glove
chewing gum
aluminum
trademark

major league
minor league
rookie
statistics
earned run average
batting average
won-lost percentage
fielding percentage
errors
assists

Writing Ideas

Here are some ideas to help incorporate writing in a unit study. Choose one or two and watch what happens!

1. Have each student identify two or three favorite baseball players, preferably from different teams. Now, have the student compose a letter to each of these players. They can ask for an autographed photograph or enclose their baseball card and ask the player to sign it and return it in the self-addressed and stamped envelope. Many times, the players will do this for children and it is such a thrill!

2. Try having the students compose a letter to each of their favorite teams and explain that they are doing a unit study about baseball and to please send any helpful information, posters, brochures, etc. We wrote to ALL of the teams and got a great response! Some teams sent team photos, or team player cards or bumper stickers, and on and on. It is so exciting to wait for the mail during these letter-writing adventures!

3. Another writing idea is to have the student compose or dictate a story about their first day as a professional baseball player. Some variations of this idea include story topics like "My Day as a Bat Boy/Girl", or "I Rode in the Limo with Cal Ripkin" (or his favorite team player).

4. If the student is playing on a baseball team during this baseball unit, consider having him keep a journal about their team experiences, day by day. He can include descriptions of practice sessions, pointers that the coaches give him, great or lousy hits he had and why, as well as comments about the games and his own performances. This should make for some interesting reading in a few years, particularly if he keeps this journal throughout his years of playing baseball.

5. Older students can do some reporting on various aspects of the game and/or its history that hold their interest. For example, they might want to look into baseball history. They could write to the various baseball museums and teams to see what kind of information they can collect, and then report on their findings. Girls that are interested in baseball and softball might be interested in investigating women's professional baseball, as well as looking into the history of the women's league that developed during World War II.

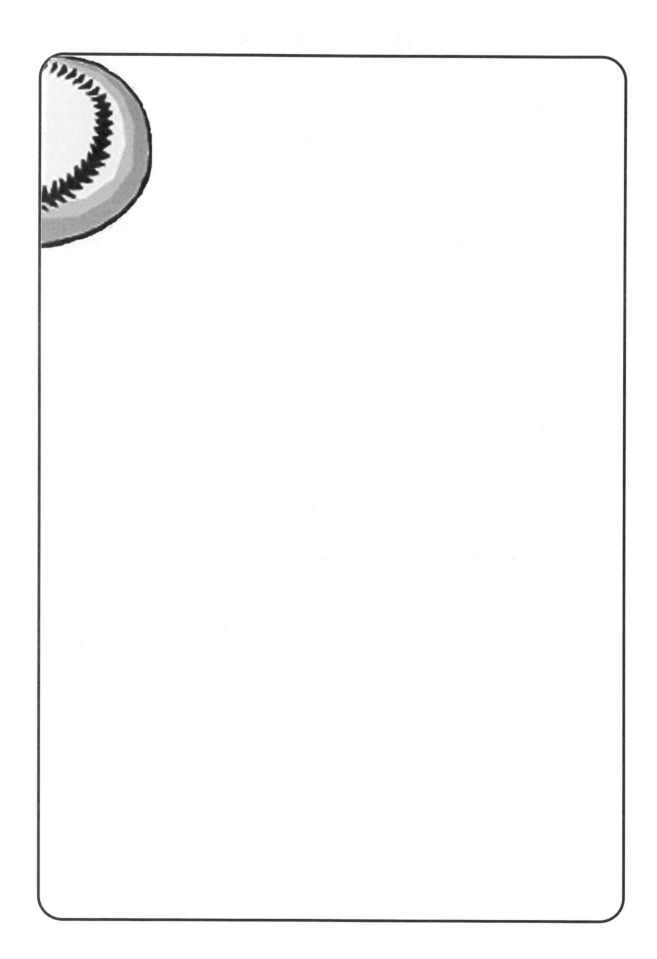

Activity Ideas

Activities are a great way to reinforce the material that we learn. They provide important hands-on learning. This allows the student to have fun and be challenged at the same time. Here are some activity resources and ideas that we found to use with this unit:

1. Many of the major and minor league baseball parks offer regular tours of their facilities. While on vacation or during a weekend trip, consider a tour of one of these parks—it is great fun and the perspective on the size of the facility and actually "being there where the players sit" is very exciting for fans of ALL ages! If interested, contact the Public Relations department of the team park that you are interested in—it might help or save money to get a group together for a tour.

2. If you live in a region that has some baseball equipment or uniform manufacturers nearby, consider calling to see if a tour is available. Some of the items of interest might include: baseballs, gloves, bats, baseball jackets, cleats, baseball caps, batting helmets, baseball jackets, athletic shoes, training equipment and so on. Many of the manufacturers and their addresses and phone numbers are listed in **The Kids' Complete Baseball Catalogue,** by Eric Weiner and published by Silver Burdett Press (ISBN 0-671-70197-5).

3. Try to have the student build a model of a baseball park, using building blocks, construction-type blocks or possibly making one from modeling clay or construction paper. The older students can get the dimensions of their favorite ballpark and build scale models.

4. Using some of the baseball math learned in the unit, have the students track the statistics of some of their favorite players and teams. They can keep a journal of the information as the unit progresses.

5. Using a book on science and sports (like **Sportsworks** by the Ontario Science Center, see **Reference Resources**), study the various aspects of science as it applies to sports. This particular book is filled with fun activities that help explain the basic principles involved.

6. Use a United States map to track the travels of the favorite teams while they are on the road. Use this opportunity to study and learn more about states, rivers and other points of geography that the teams will come across during their travels.

Activity Resources

1. For a fun brochure with color photos of baseball park prints, write:

Bill Goff, Inc.
P.O. Box 977
Kent, CT 06757

Request a catalog/brochure about his baseball art products. Bill is an artist that specializes in baseball stadium art prints. He carries his own prints, along with the stadium and baseball art prints of other sports artists. The catalog has smaller pictures of the prints that he carries, showing all the famous baseball parks of yesterday and today. Reading it is a great way to get a glimpse of the history of baseball through the artists' eyes, and perhaps help the student begin to learn more about art collecting and prints.

2. For an interesting collection of photos and descriptions of baseball collectibles, write to:

National Pastime
The Fine Art of Baseball
81 Main Street
Cooperstown, NY 13326

Request their latest brochure and then enjoy the "Vintage Memorabilia" and other collectibles depicted. They also carry some great baseball T-shirts and other baseball attire. Just the pictures of vintage photos they have available of famous players, teams, and parks were fascinating!

3. To get an interesting information packet about the Baseball Hall of Fame, write to:

National Baseball Hall of Fame and Museum
Box 590
Cooperstown, NY 13326
This museum is a popular tourist attraction and offers a vast library on baseball matters, as well as a baseball gift shop.

4. Also, consider having your softball enthusiasts contact the following for information about softball in America:

National Softball Hall of Fame and Museum
2801 Northeast 50th Street
Oklahoma City, OK 73111

Team Resources

Listed below are the addresses and phone numbers of the major league baseball teams. We wrote to all of them, requesting information to prepare a teaching unit on baseball. We received a variety of letters, baseball cards, photographs, bumper stickers and many other interesting resources from the teams and the major league baseball offices. We also learned that individuals can write to some of the team players at the addresses below, and ask for a signed photograph or other information. Have fun and enjoy your responses!

American League
350 Park Avenue
New York, NY 10022
(212) 339-7600

Baltimore Orioles
333 W. Camden St.
Baltimore, MD 21201
(410) 685-9800

Boston Red Sox
Fenway Park
Boston, MA 02215
(617) 267-9440

California Angels
P.O. Box 2000
Anaheim, CA 92803
(714) 937-7200

Chicago White Sox
333 W. 35th Street
Chicago, Ill 60616
(312) 924-1000

Cleveland Indians
2401 Ontario Street
Cleveland, OH 44115
(216) 420-4200

National League
350 Park Avenue
New York, NY 10022
(212) 339-7700

Atlanta Braves
P.O. Box 4064
Atlanta, GA 30303
(404) 522-7630

Chicago Cubs
1060 W. Addison St.
Chicago, IL 60613
(312) 404-2827

Cincinnati Reds
100 Riverfront Stadium
Cincinnati, OH 45202
(513) 421-4510

Colorado Rockies
1700 Broadway, Ste. 2100
Denver, CO 80290
(303) 292-0200

Florida Marlins
2267 N.W. 199th Street
Miami, FL 33056
(305) 626-7400

Detroit Tigers
2121 Trumbull Avenue
Detroit, MI 48216
(313) 924-1000

Kansas City Royals
P.O. Box 419969
Kansas City, MO 64141
(816) 921-2200

Milwaukee Brewers
P.O. Box 3099
Milwaukee, WI 53201
(414) 933-4114

Minnesota Twins
501 Chicago Ave., S.
Minneapolis, MN 55415
(612) 375-1366

New York Yankees
Yankee Stadium
Bronx, NY 10451
(718) 293-4300

Oakland Athletics
Oakland Coliseum
Oakland, CA 94621
(510) 638-4900

Seattle Mariners
P.O. Box 4100
Seattle, WA 98104
(206) 628-3555

Texas Rangers
P.O. Box 90111
Arlington, TX 76004
(817) 273-5222

Houston Astros
P.O. Box 288
Houston, TX 77001
(713) 799-9500

Los Angeles Dodgers
1000 Elysian Park Ave.
Los Angeles, CA 90012
(213) 224-1500

Montreal Expos
P.O. Box 500, Station M
Montreal, Quebec H1V 3P2
(514) 253-3434

New York Mets
Shea Stadium
Flushing, NY 11368
(718) 507-6387

Philadelphia Phillies
P.O. Box 7575
Philadelphia, PA 19101
(215) 463-6000

Pittsburgh Pirates
600 Stadium Circle
Pittsburgh, PA 15212
(412) 323-5000

St. Louis Cardinals
250 Stadium Circle
St. Louis, MO 63102
(314) 421-3060

San Diego Padres
P.O. Box 2000
San Diego, CA 92112
(619) 283-4494

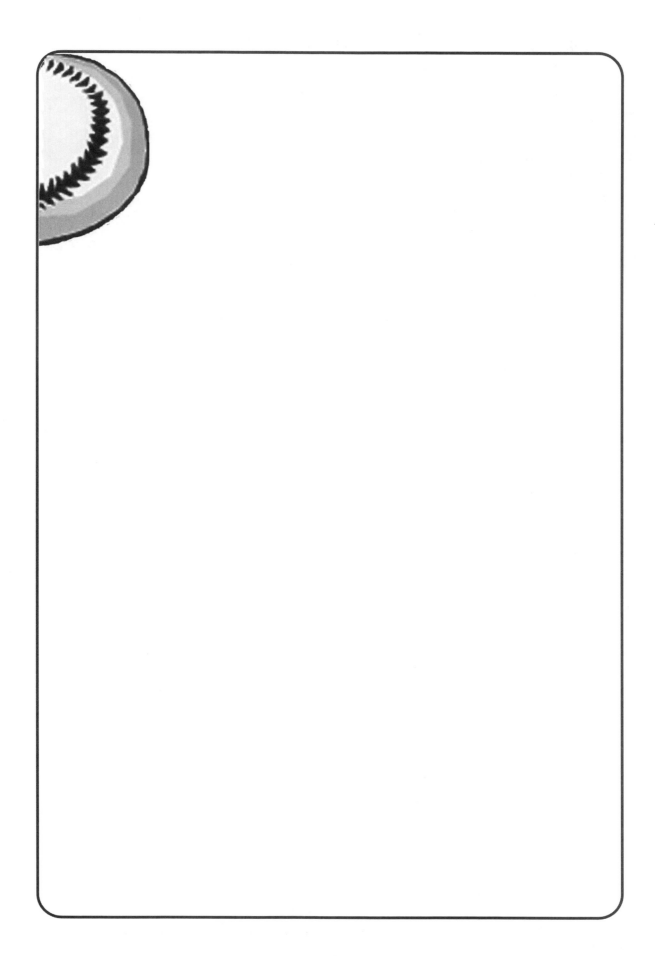

Toronto Blue Jays
1 Blue Jays Way, #3200
Toronto, Ontario M5V 1J1
(416) 341-1000

San Francisco Giants
Candlestick Park
San Francisco, CA 94124
(415) 468-3700

EXPANSION TEAMS:

Tampa Bay Devil Rays
1 Stadium Drive
St. Petersburg, FL 33705

Arizona Diamondbacks
P.O. Box 2095
Phoenix, AZ 85001

Job Opportunities

Here is a list of jobs that involve baseball. There are others that I'm sure you will identify, but these are some of the main ones that we investigated during our unit study.

Team manager	Official scorer
Baseball player	Equipment manager
Coach	Clubhouse manager/crew
Team owner	Bat boy/girl
Ground-crew member	Ticket seller
Athletic trainer	Ticket taker
Team physician	Ticket sales manager
Equipment manager	General manager
Sportscaster	Stadium security
News reporter/writer	Game announcer
Statistician	Photographer
Marketing manager	Control room terminal operator
Stadium usher	Video equipment manager
Souvenir vendor	Audio engineer
Concession manager/worker	Video engineer
Umpire	First aid nurse/EMT

For more information about these jobs or others that may be interesting, go to the reference librarian in the public library and ask for publications on careers. Some that we recommend are:

The Encyclopedia of Careers and Vocational Guidance,
published by J. G. Ferguson Publishing Company, Chicago.

Occupational Outlook Handbook, published by the U.S. Department of Labor, Bureau of Labor Statistics. It presents detailed information on 250 occupations that employ the vast majority of workers. Describes the nature of the work, training and educational requirements, working conditions and earnings potential.

Room Decorations

Consider decorating with baseball and softball items, like team pennants, drawings of baseball parks, pictures of favorite players from the newspaper, etc. Here are some of our ideas, which will hopefully stir up your family's imagination!

1.   Try putting up team pennants around the room. Instead of purchasing pennants, have the students create and draw their own on poster board and color them with markers.

2.   Draw or have the students draw a baseball diamond on poster board (to scale, if possible). They should label the positions, dimensions and areas of the field. The diamond can be either a replica of a professional field or perhaps your neighborhood ball park. Then, hang the poster up on the wall!

3.   Have students write to their favorite teams and baseball players, requesting baseball information, team photos, etc. Then, put the information that they receive around the room or on a "baseball" bulletin board.

4.   Use the sports section of your newspaper and have the students clip favorite player action shots. Display these in your room.

5.   Create a wall chart that shows the games of the seasons, team standings, schedules, etc—any information for the season that your students are interested in tracking. This way, they can update the chart on a daily basis and enjoy watching the season develop.

6.   Get a wall-size U.S. map and put it up in your school room. Place some kind of a marker at each team's home location and try to help the students learn the cities and states as their favorite team "moves" around the map to play the season games. This is great for geography lessons!

Videos

While learning about baseball, there are many great shows and videos available that relate to the sport and the players. Many of the items can be obtained through your local library or video store.

First, check at your local library and see which videos they have in their collection. We found some great ones about pitching, playing, catching, throwing and the basics of the game. Some of our favorites were those by baseball greats who shared tips and methods. There are also several series available for Little League play.

In addition, there are many great documentaries available on Public Broadcasting Stations and through the library—like the series *"Baseball"*. There are also several episodes of Reading Rainbow that cover baseball and sports. Many libraries maintain copies of Reading Rainbow episodes, usually in the Juvenile/Young Adult Reference section.

Questar Videos has also produced several videos that will add interest to your unit study. Some libraries carry these titles, or you can order them from Great Christian Books, 229 S. Bridge St., P.O. Box 8000, Elkton, MD 21922-8000, (800) 775-5422. Some titles to consider include:

America in Sports, which contains sport highlights from old newsreels and covers many types of sports through history.
Babe Ruth
America's Classic Ballparks
Baseball's Greatest Memories, Myths & Legends

There is a series of videos from Paramount that is available on home video, called *The Bad News Bears, The Bad News Bears in Breaking Training* and *The Bad News Bears Go to Japan,* about a rag-tag Little League team and their adventures. Focus on the Family also produces a movie in the "McGee and Me!"video series titled *Take Me Out of the Ballgame.*

Moody Science Adventures produces a video entitled *"The Wonder of You"* that explores the amazing human machine.

In addition to the various videos available, this unit study topic also offers the opportunity to see baseball action live through television or in person. We have watched many games, tried out our own score-keeping while watching the games and had a great time.

Games and Software

Games are a great way to reinforce the material that we learn. We have fun, while reviewing important information and concepts around the kitchen table or on the computer. The software listed here is just a small sample of what is available. While this book was being written several new games and software packages were in development for release in the near future, and all sound very exciting! Check around at your local toy and software stores to find out the latest introductions.

Baseball Legends Card Game (fun for all ages), distributed by:
Aristoplay
P.O. Box 7529
Ann Arbor, Michigan 48107
(800) 634-7738

For real baseball fans, the National Baseball Hall of Fame carries many games in its catalog. To obtain a copy of the most recent catalog, write or call: National Baseball of Hall Of Fame, P.O. Box 590, Cooperstown, NY 13326. (607) 547-2445. Some of the titles include:

1876 Centennial Baseball Game. (Ages 9 and up). A board game that is all about "real" baseball from the "Good Old Days".
Major League Baseball Game. (Ages 9 and up). A board game for trivia buffs.

Software:

Tony LaRussa BASEBALL, produced by Strategic Simulations, Inc. (Ages 8 and up). This game is in an arcade format. It gives the game-player some team management capabilities.
Hardball IV, by Accolade. (Ages 8 and up). This game is an arcade game representation of baseball.
Front Page Sports Baseball, by Sierra. (Ages 11 and up.) This game is for an older player, and involves more team management, statistics, etc.

Field Trip Ideas

There are so many field trips that can be enjoyed while learning about baseball and softball that it is hard to list all of the ones that you might want to consider. Please use this list to get started planning some field trips, then let your imagination identify others that may be in your area.

1. Consider taking a field trip to a local baseball park during a time when the field is not in use. Take along a long measuring tape and let the students measure the distances around the bases and the distance between the pitcher's mound and home plate. Have them run from home to first base, as if they had hit the ball, and let them time each other on the run to first. Use the opportunity to let them play some catch if time permits, to get a "feel" for the field and warm-ups.

2. Attend a local baseball or softball game, whether the team is made up of youngsters or is a minor league team. Have the students keep score using standard score sheets. They should track each play of the game, as well as the other important statistics. The next morning, have them compare their scoring results with those listed in the sports section of the local newspaper.

3. If your students are interested in baseball collectibles, such as baseball cards, take them to a baseball card and collectible shop. This will allow them to see the wide range of cards available, the condition of the various cards, the resale value of collected cards and collection principles in action.

4. From time to time, there may be autographing parties by baseball players at the local mall or sporting goods stores. Watch for these and take your students to see the players and get their autographs. Perhaps have them think of one thing that they would like to ask a player at the signing, if they get a chance. What a thrill to be able to ask their questions and get answers, too!

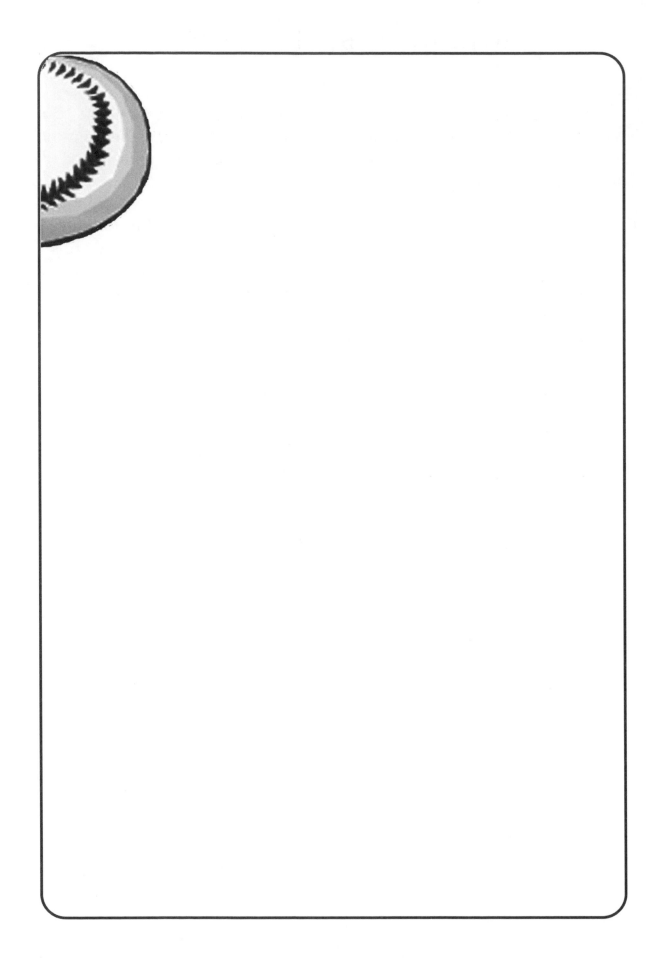

Subject Search Words

This list of **SUBJECT** search words has been included to help you with this unit study. To find material about baseball, go to the card catalog or computerized holdings catalog in your library and look up:

General Words	*People*
baseball	Lou Gehrig
softball	Dave Dravecky
batting	Cy Young
catching	Christy Mathewson
pitching	Frank Robinson
fielding	Jimmie Foxx
World Series	Babe Ruth
Little League	Billy Sunday
sports	Brooks Robinson
Major league baseball	Nolan Ryan
Minor league baseball	Mickey Mantle
Farm teams	Dale Murphy
Umpire	Dave Winfield
Baseball parks	Dizzy Dean
throwing	Roger Hornsby
baseball players	Walter Johnson
baseball statistics	Jackie Robinson
baseball leagues	Jim Abbott
baseball history	Rickey Henderson
baseball card collecting	Roy Campanella
baseball teams	Roberto Clemente
sports science	Willie Mays
Cooperstown	Willie Stargell
most valuable player	Yogi Berra
baseball managers	Hank Aaron
opening day ceremony	Johnny Bench
baseball humor	Ty Cobb
	Joe DiMaggio
	Albert Spalding

Trivia Questions

These questions have been included for fun and will reinforce some of the material that you might read during this study. Enjoy the search for answers, and then compare them with the answers that we found, located on page 67.

1. What legendary baseball player was called the "Flying Dutchman"?

2. What legendary player is known for refusing to play baseball games on Sunday?

3. Where did the bullpen get its name?

4. What great pitcher (who pitched until he was age 62) was known for his advice "If your stomach disputes you, lie down and pacify it with cool thoughts"?

5. What Native American Olympic competitor began his athletic career in minor league baseball before competing and winning in the decathlon and the pentathlon? He later left baseball to play football and eventually was elected to the Pro Football Hall of Fame.

6. What pitcher had a clause in his contract stating that he would not play ball on Jewish High Holy Days?

7.   What was the first year that the World Series was televised?

8.   When and where was the first major league night game played?

9.   When was the rule passed that players would wear protective helmets when batting?

10. Who is known for developing the minor leagues as "farm teams" for the major leagues?

11. Who wrote the poem "Casey at the Bat"?

Trivia Answers

1. What legendary baseball player was called the "Flying Dutchman"?

   Honus Wagner

2. What legendary player is known for refusing to play baseball games on Sunday?

   Christy Mathewson

3. Where did the bullpen get its name?

   In the early days of professional baseball, pitchers would warm up by the outfield walls, which often had a billboard ad for Bull Durham chewing tobacco

4. What great pitcher (who pitched until he was age 62) was known for his advice "If your stomach disputes you, lie down and pacify it with cool thoughts"?

   Satchel Paige

5. What Native American Olympic competitor began his athletic career in minor league baseball before competing and winning in the decathlon and the pentathlon? He later left baseball to play football and eventually was elected to the Pro Football Hall of Fame.

   Jim Thorpe

6. What pitcher had a clause in his contract stating that he would not play ball on Jewish High Holy Days?

   Sandy Koufax

7. What was the first year that the World Series was televised?

   1947

8. When and where was the first major league night game played?

On May 24, 1935 at Crosley Field in Cincinnati

9. When was the rule passed that players would wear protective helmets when batting?

1971

10. Who is known for developing the minor leagues as "farm teams" for the major leagues?

Branch Rickey

11. Who wrote the poem "Casey at the Bat"?

Ernest Lawrence Thayer

Reference Resources
History

Here are some of the reference resources that will be helpful during your study of baseball. These are just a few of the ones available, so use the Subject Word List to locate others through your library.

A Promise Kept: The Story of the Founding of Little League Baseball, by Carl Stotz. Young Adult—Grades 7 - 12. Published by Zebrowski Historical Services, R.R. 1 Box 53, Bloomingburg, NY 12721.

A Whole New Ball Game: The Story Behind a League of Their Own, by Sue Macy. Grades 7 and up. Published by Henry Holt & Co., 4419 West, 1980 South, Salt Lake City, UT 84104. (800) 488-5233.

Black Diamond: The Story of Negro Baseball Leagues, by Patricia McKissack. Grades 3 - 9. Published by Scholastic, Inc., P.O. Box 7502, Jefferson City, MO 65102. (800) 325-6149.

Great Moments in Baseball, by Bill Gutman. (Sports Illustrated Series). Grades 5 and up. Published by Pocket Books, Division of Simon & Schuster, Paramount Publishing, 200 Old Tappan Rd., Old Tappan, NJ 07675. (800) 223-2348.

Playing America's Game: The Story of Negro League Baseball, by Michael Cooper. Grades 4 - 7. Published by Dutton Children's Books, Division of Penguin USA, 375 Hudson St., New York, NY 10014. (212) 366-2000.

The Story of Baseball, by Lawrence S. Ritter. Grades 3 and up. Published by William Morrow and Company, 39 Plymouth St., Fairfield, NJ 07004. (800) 843-9389.

Who Invented the Game?, by Ken Burns. (Baseball, the American Epic Series). Grades 3 - 7. Published by Knopf, Subsidiary of Random House, 400 Hahn Rd., Westminster, MD 21157. (800) 733-3000.

Who Invented Baseball?, by Paul Walker. Grades 4 and up. Published by Random House Books for Young Readers, 400 Hahn Rd., Westminster, MD 21157. (800) 733-3000.

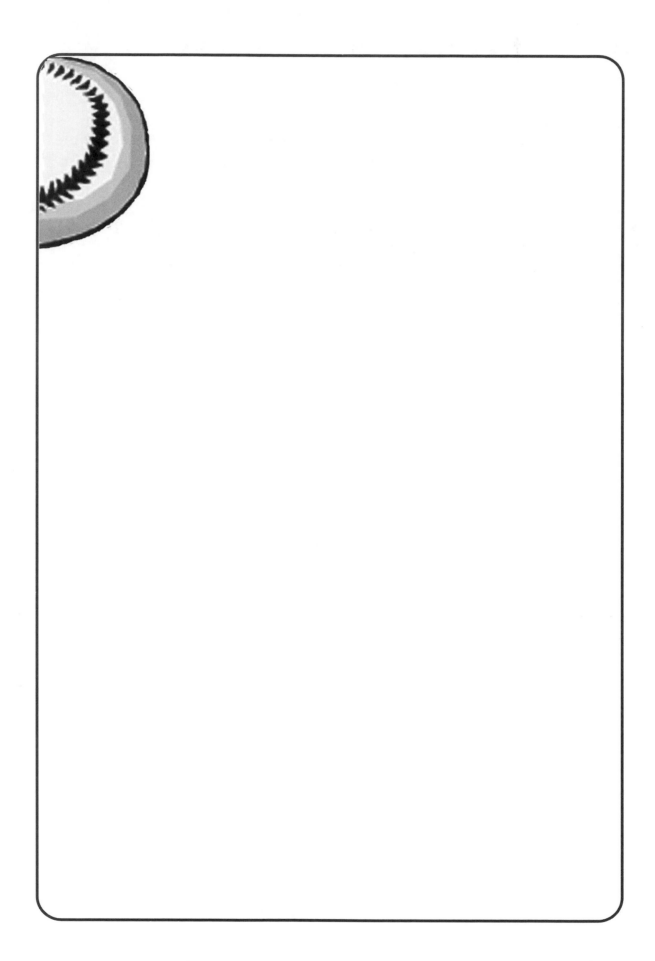

Reference Resources
The Game

All About Baseball, by George Sullivan. Grades 3 and up. Published by Putnam Berkeley Group, 200 Madison Ave., New York, NY 10016. (800) 631-8571.

Baseball, by Bill Gutman. (Go For It Series). Grades 3 - 8. Published by Marshall Cavendish Corporation, 99 White Plains Rd., P.O. Box 2001, Tarrytown, NY 10591-9001. (800) 821-9881.

Baseball & Softball, by Paul Gregory. (Play the Game Series). Young Adult— Grades 10 - 12. Published by Sterling Publishing Co., 387 Park Ave. S., New York, NY 10016. (800) 367-9692.

Basic Baseball Strategy: An Introduction for Young Players, by S. H. Freeman. Grades 5 and up. Published by Doubleday & Company, Garden City, NY. This is an older book, ©1965, but has a wonderful presentation about strategy, with illustrations that are great!

Get Inside Baseball, by Paul Almonte. (Get Inside Series). Grades 4 - 6. Published by Silver Moon, distributed by August House, P.O. Box 3223, Little Rock, AR 72203-3223. (501) 372-5450.

Hitting, by Jay Feldman. (The Official Major League Baseball Books). Grades 5 and up. Published by Simon & Schuster Trade, 200 Old Tappan Rd., Old Tappan, NJ 07675. (800) 223-2348.

Jerry Koosman's Guide for Young Pitchers, by Jerry Koosman. Grades 2 - 6. Published by Young Creations, P.O. Box 27, New Germany, MN 99367.

Little League's Official How-to-Play Baseball Handbook, by Peter Kruetzer. Published by Bantam Doubleday Dell, 2451 S. Wolf Rd., Des Plains, IL 60018. (800) 323-9872.

Pitching, by Dan Schlossberg. Grades 5 and up. (The Official MLB Books). Published by Simon & Schuster Trade, 200 Old Tappan Rd., Old Tappan, NJ 07675. (800) 223-2348.

Red Foley's Best Baseball Book, by Red Foley. Grades 4 - 7. Published by Simon & Schuster Trade, 200 Old Tappan Rd., Old Tappan, NJ 07675. (800) 223-2348.

The Baseball Book, by Zander Hollander. Grades 5 and up. Published by Random House Books for Young Readers, 400 Hahn Rd., Westminster, MD 21157. (800) 733-3000.

The Major League Way to Play Baseball, (The Official Major League Baseball Books). Grades 3 and up. Published by Simon & Schuster Trade, 200 Old Tappan Rd., Old Tappan, NJ 07675. (800) 223-2348.

The Easy Baseball Book, by Jonah Kalb. Grades 2 - 5. Published by Houghton Mifflin Co., Individual/Trade Division, 181 Ballardvale Rd., Wilmington, MA 01887 (800) 225-3362

This is Baseball, by Margaret Blackstone. Grades Preschool - K. Published by Henry Holt & Co., 4419 West, 1980 South, Salt Lake City, UT 94104. (800) 488-5233.

Disciple of a Master (How to Hit a Baseball to Your Potential) Grades 7 - 12. Published by Line Drive Publishing, 113 Pleasant St., Hanover, MA 02339. (617) 878-5035.

The First Book of Baseball, by Marty Appel. Grades 4 and up. Published by Crown Publishers, Inc., Division of Random House, 201 East 50th St., New York, NY 10022. (800) 726-0600.

A Warm Up For Little League Baseball, by Morris Shirts. Grades 3 - 6. Published by Pocket Books, a Division of Simon & Schuster, 200 Old Tappan Rd., Old Tappan, NJ 07675. (800) 223-2336.

Everyone Wins at Tee Ball, by Henry & Janet Grosshandler. Grades K - 3. Published by Dutton Children's Books, Division of Penguin USA, 375 Hudson St., New York, NY 10014. (212) 366-2000.

Reference Resources
Players

A Boy & His Baseball: The Dave Dravecky Story, by Judy Gire. Published by Zondervan, Division of HarperCollins Publications, Order Processing-B36, 5300 Patterson Ave. SE, Grand Rapids, MI 49530. (800) 727-1309.

Baseball Legends Series, by Norm Macht. Grades 3 and up. Published by Chelsea House Publishers, 1974 Sproul Rd., Suite 400, P.O. Box 914, Broomall, PA 19008. (800) 848-2665. Also, these books on other players are listed in this series by the same author and publisher:

Babe Ruth
Cy Young
Christy Mathewson
Frank Robinson
Jimmie Foxx

Babe Ruth: One of Baseball's Greatest, by Guernsey Van Riper, Jr. (Childhood of Famous Americans Series). Grades 2 - 6. Published by Simon & Schuster, owners of Macmillan Children's Books, 200 Old Tappan Rd., Old Tappan, NJ 07675. (800) 257-5755.

Baseball Heroes Series. Grades 3 and up. Published by Rourke Corporation, P.O. Box 3328, Vero Beach, FL (407) 465-4575. Also, these additional titles are listed in this series by the same publisher:

Base Stealers
M.V.P.
Batting Champ
Home Run Leaders

Baseball's Best: Five True Stories, by Andrew Gutelle. (Step Into Reading Books). Grades 2 - 4. Published by Random House Books for Young Readers, 400 Hahn Rd., Westminster, MD 21157. (800) 733-3000.

Billy Sunday: Baseball Preacher, by Fern N. Stocker. (Preteen Biography Series). Grades 2 - 7. Published by Moody Press, 820 N. LaSalle Blvd., Chicago, IL 60610. (800) 678-8812.

Baseball Legends Series, by Rick Wolff. Grades 3 and up. Published by Chelsea House Publishers, 1974 Sproul Rd., Suite 400, P.O. Box 914, Broomall, PA 19008. (800) 848-2665. In the series, by the same author and publisher:

Brooks Robinson
Mickey Mantle

Comeback, by Dave Dravecky. Published by Zondervan, Division of HarperCollins Publications, Order Processing-B36, 5300 Patterson Ave. SE, Grand Rapids, MI 49530. (800) 727-1309.

Dale Murphy: Baseball's Gentle Giant, by Patricia Martin. (Reaching Your Goal Books). Grades 1 - 4. Published by Rourke Corporation, P.O. Box 3328, Vero Beach, FL (407) 465-4575.

Dave Winfield, by Judy Monroe. (Sports Close-Ups Series). Grades 5 - 6. Published by Simon & Schuster, owners of Macmillan Children's Books, 200 Old Tappan Rd., Old Tappan, NJ 07675. (800) 223-2348.

Baseball Legends Series, by Jack Kavanaugh. Grades 3 and up. Published by Chelsea House Publishers, 1974 Sproul Rd., Suite 400, Broomall, PA 19008. (800) 848-2665. In this series by the same author and publisher:

Dizzy Dean
Roger Hornsby
Walter Johnson

Hit Men (Baseball's Best Series). Grades 1 and up. Published by Simon & Schuster Trade, 200 Old Tappan Rd., Old Tappan, NJ 07675. (800) 223-2348.

Home Run Kings (Baseball's Best Series). Grades 1 and up. Published by Simon & Schuster Trade, 200 Old Tappan Rd., Old Tappan, NJ 07675. (800) 223-2348.

Jackie Robinson, by John Grabowski. (Baseball Legends Series). Grades 3 and up. Published by Chelsea House Publishers, 1974 Sproul Rd., Suite 400, Broomall, PA 19008. (800) 848-2665.

Jim Abbott: Star Pitcher, by Bill Gutman. Grades 4 - 7. Published by Houghton Mifflin Co., Individual/Trade, 181 Ballardvale Rd., Wilmington, MA 01887 (800) 225-3362

Jim Abbott: Beating the Odds, by Rick Johnson. (Taking Part Series). Grades 3 and up. Published by Simon & Schuster, owners of Macmillan Children's Books, 200 Old Tappan Rd., Old Tappan, NJ 07675. (800) 223-2348.

Jim Abbott: Star Pitcher, by Bill Gutman. Grades 3 - 6. Published by Millbrook Press, 2 Old New Milford Rd., Brookfield, CT 06804. (800) 462-4703.

Little Big Leaguers: Amazing Boyhood Stories of Today's Baseball Stars, by Bruce Nash. Grades 4 - 7. Published by Simon & Schuster Trade, 200 Old Tappan Rd., Old Tappan, NJ 07675. (800) 223-2348.

More Little Big Leaguers: Amazing Boyhood Stories of Today's Baseball Stars, by Bruce Nash. Grades 1 and up. Published by Simon & Schuster Trade, 200 Old Tappan Rd., Old Tappan NJ 07675 (800) 223-2348.

Rickey Henderson: Record Stealer, by Ann Bauleke. (Sports Achiever Series). Grades 4 - 9. Published by Lerner Publications, 241 First Ave. N., Minneapolis, MN 55401. (800) 328-4929.

Roy Campanella, by James Tackach. (Baseball Legends Series). Grades 3 and up. Published by Chelsea House Publishers, 1974 Sproul Rd., Suite 400, P.O. Box 914, Broomall, PA 19008. (800) 848-2665.

Sluggers! Twenty-Seven of Baseball's Greatest, by George Sullivan. Grades 3 and up. Published by Simon & Schuster, owners of Macmillan Children's Books, 200 Old Tappan Rd., Old Tappan, NJ 07675. (800) 223-2348.

Story of Roberto Clemente, by Jim O'Connor. Grades 4 - 7. Published by Bantam, Doubleday, Dell Publishing Co., 2451 S. Wolf Rd., Des Plains, IL 60018. (800) 323-9872.

When You Can't Come Back, by Dave Dravecky. Published by Zondervan, Division of HarperCollins Publications, Order Processing-B36, 5300 Patterson Ave. S.E., Grand Rapids, MI 49530. (800) 727-1309.

Willie Mays, Young Superstar, by Louis Sabin. Grades 4 - 6. Published by Troll Associates, Penguin USA, 375 Hudson St., New York, NY 10014. (800) 331-4624.

Willie Stargell, by Mike Shannon. (Baseball Legends Series). Grades 3 and up. Published by Chelsea House Publishers , 1974 Sproul Rd., Suite 400, P.O. Box 914, Broomall, PA 19008. (800) 848-2665.

Yogi Berra, by Marty Appel. (Baseball Legends Series). Grades 3 and up. Published by Chelsea House Publishers, 1974 Sproul Rd., Suite 400, P.O. Box 914, Broomall, PA 19008. (800) 848-2665.

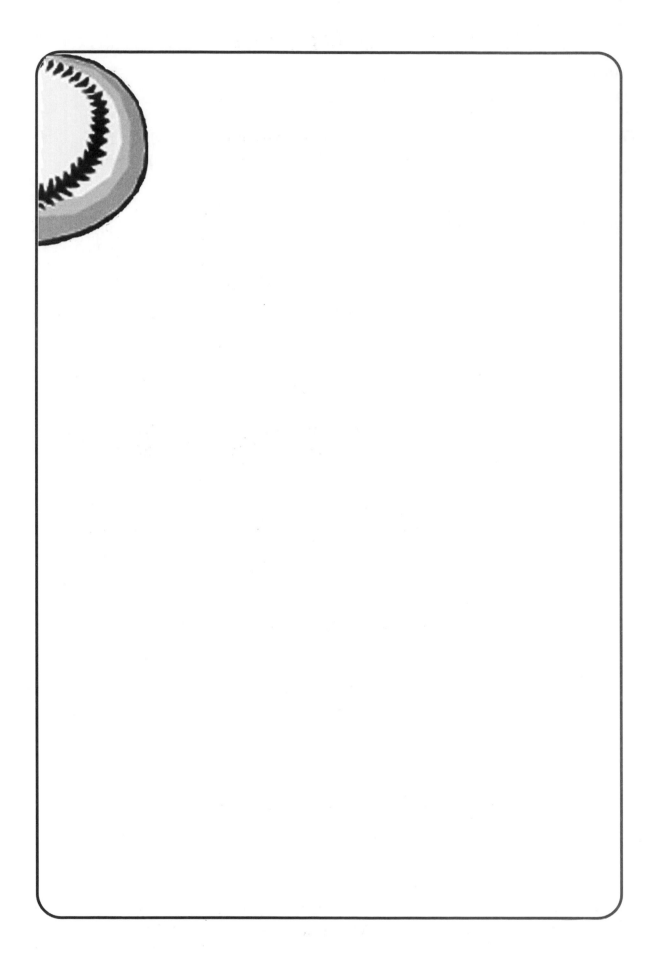

Reference Resources
Parks and Stadiums

Brooklyn Dodger Days, by Richard Rosenblum. Grades 1 - 5. Published by Simon & Schuster, owners of Macmillan Children's Books, 200 Old Tappan Rd., Old Tappan, NJ 07675. (800) 223-2348.

Fenway Park: Build It Yourself, by Len Martin. Published by Addison Wesley, 1 Jacob Way, Reading, MA 01867. (800) 447-2226.

Fields of Summer: Great American Ballparks & The Players Who Triumphed in Them, by James Tackach. Published by Random House Value, 400 Hahn Rd., Westminster, MD 21157. (800) 733-3000.

The Ballpark: One Day Behind the Scenes at a Major League Game, by William Jaspersohn. Grades 4 and up. Published by Little, Brown and Co., 200 West St., Waltham, MA 02154. (800) 759-0190. This is an older book, ©1980, but does a good job of describing what really happens at the ball park behind the scenes.

Reference Resources
Careers

Career Opportunities in the Sports Industry, by Shelly Field. Young Adult—Grades 9 - 12. Published by Facts on File, 11 Penn Plaza, 15th Floor, New York, NY 10001. (800) 322-8755.

I Can Be a Baseball Player, by Carol Greene. Grades K - 3. Published by Children's Press, P.O. Box 1331, Danbury, CT 06813. (800) 621-1115.

Sports: Careers in Sports, by Staci Bonner. (Now Hiring Series). Grades 5 - 6. Published by Simon & Schuster, owners of Macmillan Children's Books, 866 Third Ave., 25th Floor, New York, NY 10022. (800) 223-2348.

You Can Do It! Careers in Baseball, by Howard Blumenthal. Published by Little, Brown and Co., 200 West St., Waltham, MA 02154. (800) 759-0190.

Reference Resources
Math

Baseball By The Numbers: How Statistics are Collected, What They Mean, & How They Reveal the Game, by Willie Runquist. Published by McFarland & Co., Box 611, Jefferson, NC 28640. (910) 246-4460.

Baseball Math: Grandslam Activities and Projects for Grades 4 - 8, by Christopher Jennison. Grades 4 - 8. Published by Good Year Books, a Division of HarperCollins Publishers, 1000 Keystone Industrial Park, Scranton, PA 18512. (800) 242-7737.

Play Ball: Sports Math, by Time Life editors. (I Love Math Series). Grades K - 4. Published by Time Life Publishing, 777 Duke St., Alexandria, VA 22314. (800) 621-7026.

Reading the Sports Page: A Guide to Understanding Sports Statistics, by Jeremy Feinberg. Grades 6 and up. Published by Simon & Schuster, owners of Macmillan Children's Books, 200 Old Tappan Rd., Old Tappan, NJ 07675. (800) 223-2348.

The Official Baseball Hall of Fame Scorebook, by Neil Cohen. Grades 6 and up. Published by Simon & Schuster, 200 Old Tappan Rd., Old Tappan, NJ 07675. (800) 223-2348.

Reference Resources
Science

Sportsworks, by the Ontario Science Centre. Grades 2 - 7. Published by Addison-Wesley Publishing, 1 Jacob Way, Reading, MA 01867. (800) 447-2226. (Very activity-oriented).

Sports Science for Young People, by George Barr. Grades 6 and up. Published by Dover Publications, 31 East 2nd Street, Mineola, NY 11501.

Sports Technology, by Neil Duncanson. (Technology in Action Series). Grades 5 - 7. Published by Franklin Watts, Chicago, IL. (800) 672-6672.

Experimenting With Science in Sports, by Robert Gardner. Young Adult— Grades 7 - 12. Published by Franklin Watts, Chicago, IL. (800) 672-6672.

Reference Resources
Softball

I Love Softball, by Barbara Berst. Grades 3 - 6. Published by National Lilac Publishing, 295 Sharpe Rd., Anacorte-Fidalgo Island, WA 98221.

Softball, by Bill Gutman. (Go For It Series). Grades 3 - 8. Published by Marshall Cavendish Corporation, 99 White Plains Rd., P.O. Box 20001, Tarrytown, NY 10591-9001. (800) 821-9881.

Softball is for Me, by Rosemary G. Washington. (Sports for Me Series). Grades 3 - 6. Published by Lerner Publications, 241 First Ave. N., Minneapolis, MN 55401. (800) 328-4929.

Baseball & Softball, by Paul Gregory. (Play the Game Series) Young Adult—Grades 10 - 12. Published by Sterling Publishing Co., 387 Park Ave. S., New York, NY 10016. (800) 367-9692.

Reference Resources
Card Collecting

A Kid's Guide to Collecting Baseball Cards, by Casey Childress. Grades 3 - 9. Harbinger House, P.O. Box 42948, Tucson, AZ 85733.

Baseball Card Crazy, by Trish Kennedy. Grades 4 - 6. Published by Simon & Schuster, owners of Macmillan Children's Books, 200 Old Tappan Rd., Old Tappan, NJ 07675. (800) 223-2348.

How To Profit from Baseball Card Collecting: A Basic Guide for the New Collector - Investor, by Fred Hollman. Grades Preschool - 12. Published by Reymont Associates, P.O. Box 114, New York, NY 10276. (212) 473-8031.

Start Collecting Baseball Cards, by David Platt. Grades 4 and up. Published by Running Press, 125 S. 22nd St., Philadelphia, PA 19103. (800) 345-5359.

The Grand Slam Collection: Have Fun Collecting Baseball Cards, by Jerry Ford. (Collecting Made Easy Series). Grades 5 - 12. Published by Lerner Publications, 241 First Ave. N., Minneapolis, MN 55401. (800) 328-4929.

Reference Resources
Miscellaneous

Everything Baseball ("Featuring absolutely every baseball song, poem, novel, play, movie, TV and radio show, painting, sculpture, comic strip, cartoon, and more"), by James Mote. Grades 7 and up. Published by Prentice Hall Press, 200 Old Tappan Rd., Old Tappan, NJ 07675. (800) 922-0579.

Illustrated Baseball Dictionary for Young People, by Henry Walker. Grades 4 and up. Published by Prentice Hall Press, 200 Old Tappan Rd., Old Tappan, NJ 07675. (800) 922-0579. This is an older book, ©1970, but has helped us with our baseball "lingo" quite a bit.

Louisville Slugger: The Making of a Baseball Bat, by Jan Arnow. Grades 3 - 7. Published by Pantheon Books, Division of Random House, 400 Hahn Rd., Westminster, MD 21157. (800) 733-3000.

My Baseball Book: A Write-in-Me Book for Young Players, by Tom Ettinger. Grades 3 - 7. Published by HarperCollins Children's Books, 1000 Keystone Industrial Park, Scranton, PA 18512. (800) 242-7737.

Playbook! Baseball: You Are the Manager, You Call the Shots. (Sports Illustrated for Kids Books). Grades 3 - 7. Published by Little, Brown and Co., 200 West St., Waltham, MA 02154. (800) 759-0190.

The Kids' Complete Baseball Catalogue, by Eric Weiner. Grades 5 and up. Published by Simon & Schuster Trade, 200 Old Tappan Rd., Old Tappan, NJ 07675. (800) 223-2348.

The Kids' World Almanac of Baseball, by Thomas G. Aylesworth. Grades 4 and up. Published by World Almanac, One International Blvd., Mahway, NJ 07495. (201) 529-6900.

Sports, by Tim Hammond. (Eyewitness Books). Grades 5 and up. Published by Knopf Books for Young Readers, New York. (800) 733-3000.

Spring Training, by Henry Horenstein. Grades 2 and up. Published by Simon & Schuster, owners of Macmillan Children's Books, 200 Old Tappan Rd., Old Tappan, NJ 07675. (800) 223-2348.

Reading Resources

A Century of Children's Baseball Stories, by Debra Dagavarian (Editor).
Grades 5 and up. Published by Mecklermedia Corp., 11 Ferry Ln. W.,
Westport, CT 06880. (203) 266-6967.

Paul the Pitcher, by Paul Sharp. (Rookie Reader Series) Grades Preschool - 2.
Published by Children's Press, P.O. Box 1331, Danbury, CT 06813.
(800) 621-1115.

The Macmillan Book of Baseball Stories, by Terry Egan. Grades 3 and up.
Published by Simon & Schuster, owners of Macmillan Children's Books, 200
Old Tappan Rd., Old Tappan, NJ 07675. (800) 223-2348.

Casey at the Bat: A Ballad of the Republic, Sung in the Year 1888, by Ernest
L. Thayer. Grades K - 5. Published by Putnam Berkeley Group, 390 Murray
Hill Parkway, East Rutherford, NJ 07073. (800) 631-8571.

Baseball Fever, by Johanna Hurwitz. Published by William Morrow &
Company, New York.

High Fly to Center, by Bill J. Carol. Published by Steck Vaughn, Austin, TX.

Internet Resources

Here are some interesting sites on the Internet that you might want to visit while studying this unit. Please keep in mind that these pages, like all web pages, change from time to time. I recommend that you visit each site first, before the children do, to view the content and make sure that it meets your expectations. Also, use the **Subject Key Words** as search topics on Internet search engines, to find the latest additions that might pertain to this topic. (For help getting online, I highly recommend Homeschool Guide to the Online World — ISBN 1-888306-16-5.)

Overview of the National Baseball Hall of Fame and Museum:
http://www.enews.com/bas_hall_fame/overview.html

Fellowship of Christian Athletes (FCA):
http://www.fca.org

Sports Spectrum, a Christian sports magazine:
http://www.gospelcom.net/rbc/ss

Christian Sports Flash Weekly:
http://www.gospelcom.net/gf/sf/

Instant Baseball:
http://www.InstantSports.com/baseball.html

Minor Leagues, Major Dreams:
http://www.minorleagues.com/minorleagues/

The Major League Baseball Page:
http://www.sportsnetwork.com/mlb/mlb.html

Baseball Hotlist:
http://allsports.questtech.com/NFL/baseball.html

Sports Information Server:
http://www.netgen.com/sis/sports.html

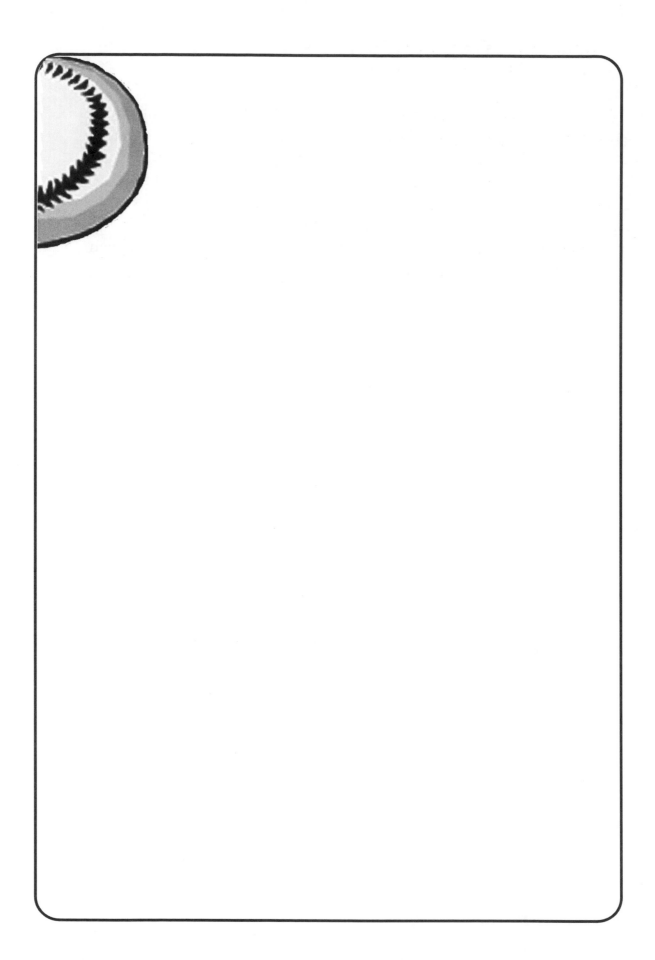

Internet Baseball Archive Web Page:
http://www.baseball.org/baseball/

Sports Outdoors - Baseball; Instructional Videos and CDS:
http://www.schoolroom.com/gift/s_base.htm

Search for Baseball Camps:
http://www.kidscamps.com/specialty/sports/baseball.html

Little League Baseball:
http://www.littleleague.org/

The Tom Seaver Museum—Main Lobby:
http://www.servtech.com/public/pnm/seaver/

Amanda Bennett's Unit Study Web Page:
http.//www.gocin.com/unit_study/

Working Outline

(This is the same outline as the one in the front of this unit study guide. However, the spacing between sections has been increased to provide working and writing room for use with the unit.)

I.   History of baseball

    A.   Early beginnings—there were many games throughout history that were ball and stick types of games

        1.   Paddleball

        2.   Trap ball

        3.   Rounders

        4.   Town Hall

        5.   Cricket

    B.   Development of the game in the nineteenth century

        1.   Developed from a children's game into a game for all ages, and particularly held the interest of men

2. Baseball as we know it today first appeared in New York at the Knickerbocker Club, under the guidance of Alexander Cartwright (1845)

    a. Diamond-shape field

    b. Bases 90 feet apart

    c. Nine-man team

    d. Three outs for each of two teams in each inning

    e. First official game under Mr. Cartwright's rule was probably played on June 19, 1846

3. The first baseball league was formed in 1858, called the National Association of Base Ball Players

4. When the Civil War broke out, the game was spread to all sections of the country by northern soldiers

5. The first professional team (salaried) was announced in 1869, the Cincinnati Red Stockings

6. The first professional baseball league, the National Association of Professional Base Ball Players was formed by the players in 1871

7. In 1876, the National League was formed

8. Innovations for the game and the spectator were developed in the late 1800's

    a. The baseball glove was invented in the late 1870's

    b. Concessions were developed in the late 1800's to satisfy the growing crowd's hunger at games—these sold hot dogs, soda pop and peanuts.

9. The rules were changed in 1884, permitting pitchers to throw overhand pitches

10. The American League was formed in 1899, became a major league in 1901

C. Development of the game in the twentieth century

    1. The National Commission for Baseball was formed in 1903 to oversee major league baseball

2.   In 1908, the song "Take Me Out to the Ball Game" was introduced

3.   Permanent baseball parks were built in the early 1900's baseball boom

4.   Baseball grew rapidly in popularity in the early 1900's

5.   The World Series began in 1903

6.   World War I broke out, and many of the professional ball players joined the military

7.   After the war, baseball's popularity came back

8.   Andrew (Rube) Foster formed the Negro National League in 1920, in response to opposition to racial integration in the major leagues

9.   In 1928, the Negro American League formed

10.   Night baseball was begun in the major leagues in 1935

11. World War II brought hard times for major league baseball. Players joined the military and shortages in transportation and rubber slowed down the growth and interest in baseball

12. In 1943, Philip Wrigley started the All-American Girls Softball League

13. In the 1940's, black players were accepted into the major leagues

14. In the 1950's, franchises began to break away from their original hometowns to move to better towns and hopefully, more income

15. As the games became televised, game times were scheduled later in the day, and baseball slowly became dependent on television

D. History of baseball leagues

1. Major Leagues

2. Minor Leagues

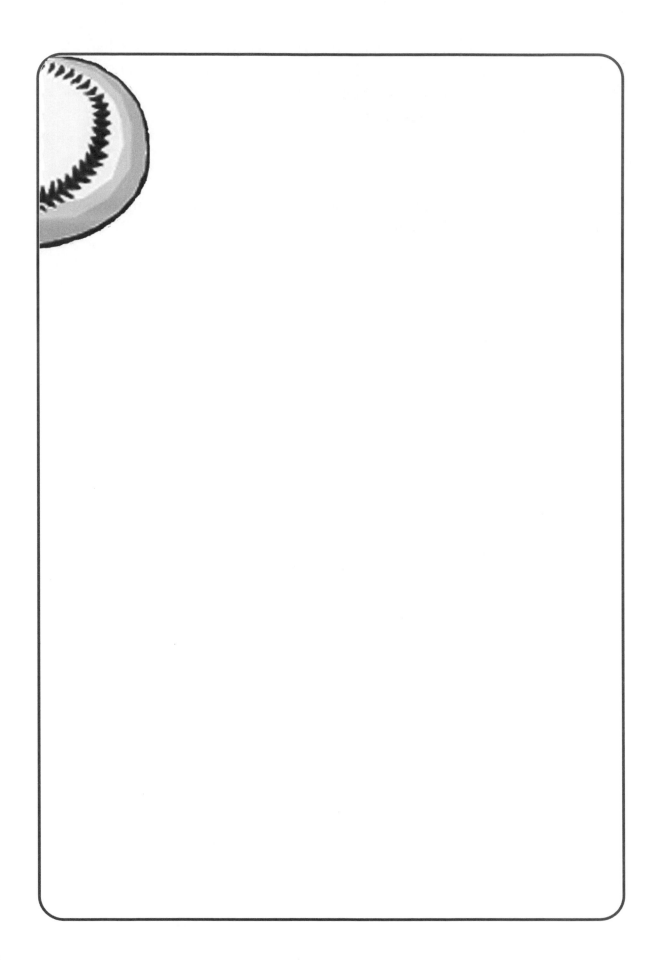

3.   All-American Girls Professional Baseball League

4.   Negro League

5.   College League

6.   Little League

7.   Grapefruit League

8.   Cactus League

II.   Baseball—the game

A.   The baseball parks

1.   Dimensions

a.   Infield is a square of 90 foot long sides

(1)   Pitcher's mound is an 18 foot circle

(2)   Pitcher's mound is 60.5 feet from home plate

b. Outfield can be of varying dimensions

2. Major League parks of yesterday and today

B. The team

1. Number of players

2. Positions

a. Pitcher

(1) Starting pitcher

(2) Relief pitcher

b. Catcher

c. Infielder

(1) First baseman

(2) Second baseman

        (3)   Third baseman

        (4)   Shortstop

    d.   Outfielder

        (1)   Left fielder

        (2)   Center fielder

        (3)   Right fielder

3.   Batting order

4.   Designated hitter

5.   Regulars and reserves

6.   The staff

    a.   Coaching staff

        b.   Athletic trainers

        c.   Team manager

C.   The game play

    1.   A major league baseball game consists of nine innings

        a.   An inning consists of each team staying at bat until they have three outs (each team has a half-inning)

        b.   Extra innings can be played if the score is tied at the end of nine innings

    2.   The teams get set for play

        a.   Home team is out in the field first

        b.   Visiting team is first at bat

        c.   Team managers choose players for each position, as well as a batting lineup

3. The pitch, the hit, and the play

    a. The pitch

        (1) Strike—three3 strikes, player is out

        (2) Foul

        (3) Ball—four balls, player walks to first base

        (4) Hit by pitch—player advances to first base

        (5) Ball is hit into play

    b. The hit

        (1) Types of hits

            (a) Bunt

            (b) Ground ball

            (c) Line drive

            (d) Fly ball

            (e) Home run

        (2) Results of hits

            (a) Fly ball is caught—player is out

            (b) One-base hit is called a single

        (c)   Two-base hit is called a double

        (d)   Three-base hit is called a triple

        (e)   Four-base hit is called a home run

    c.   The play—advancing around the bases

        (1)   Running on a hit

        (2)   Stealing bases

        (3)   On a sacrifice

4.   The umpires

    a.   Enforce the game rules

    b.   Call the pitches—strikes, fouls and fair balls

    c.   Rule whether or not the runner is safe or out

III. Science in Baseball

    A.   Reflexes and reaction times—the roles they play in hitting and catching

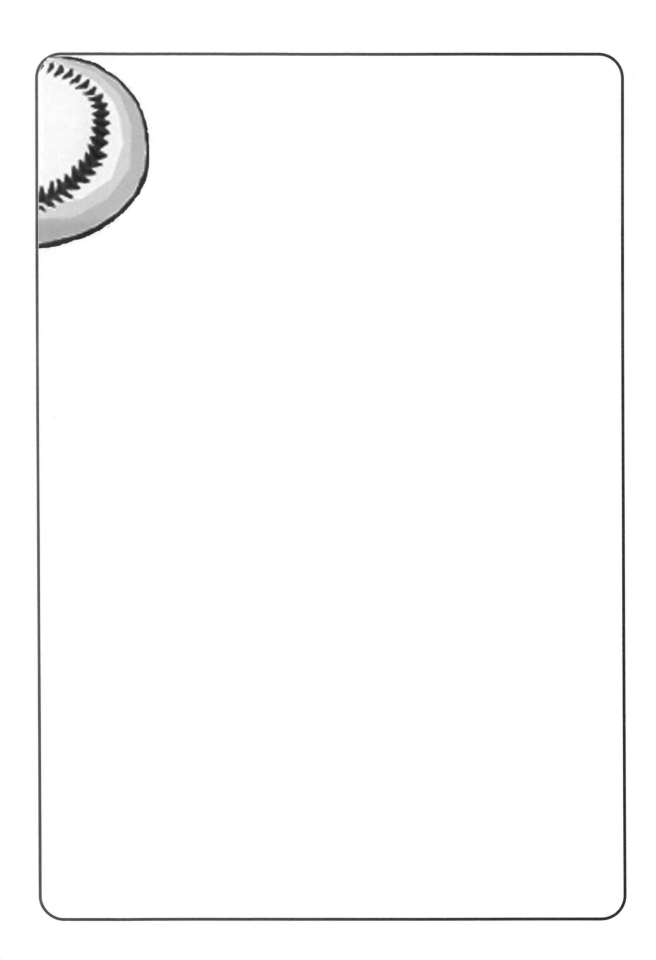

B.   Sliding into a base—using friction to help slow down to tag the base and stop

C.   Making a ball curve or "break" with spin—using aerodynamics to help change the path of a ball

D.   Leverage in baseball—the bat is a simple lever, and the load to be moved is the baseball

E.   Gravity and the role it plays in bringing a thrown ball to the ground—why a thrown ball needs to have an arc to go longer distances

F.   Rounding the bases to fight inertia—making the most of the runner's building speed while still tagging the bases using a curved path

G.   Warming up before a game—providing muscles with extra oxygen to make them stronger and able to endure more than "cold" muscles

IV.   The Major Leagues

A.   The season of play

1.   Spring Training—to prepare for the upcoming season

2. Regular season play—162 games

3. Division playoffs for each league's pennant

4. Winners of the league pennants compete in the World Series

B. The American League (East and West Divisions)

1. Baltimore Orioles— Baltimore, Maryland

2. Boston Red Sox— Boston, Massachusetts

3. California Angels—Anaheim, California

4. Chicago White Sox—Chicago, Illinois

5. Cleveland Indians—Cleveland, Ohio

6. Detroit Tigers—Detroit, Michigan

7.   Kansas City Royals—Kansas City, Missouri

8.   Milwaukee Brewers—Milwaukee, Wisconsin

9.   Minnesota Twins—Bloomington, Minnesota

10.   New York Yankees—The Bronx, New York

11.   Oakland Athletics—Oakland, California

12.   Seattle Mariners—Seattle, Washington

13.   Texas Rangers—Arlington, Texas

14.   Toronto Blue Jays—Toronto, Ontario, Canada

C.   The National League (East and West Divisions)

    1.   Atlanta Braves—Atlanta, Georgia

2.   Chicago Cubs—Chicago, Illinois

3.   Cincinnati Reds—Cincinnati, Ohio

4.   Colorado Rockies—Denver, Colorado

5.   Florida Marlins—Ft. Lauderdale/Miami, Florida

6.   Houston Astros—Houston, Texas

7.   Los Angeles Dodgers—Los Angeles, California

8.   Montreal Expos—Montreal, Quebec, Canada

9.   New York Mets—Flushing, New York

10.   Philadelphia Phillies—Philadelphia, Pennsylvania

11.   Pittsburgh Pirates—Pittsburgh, Pennsylvania

12.	St. Louis Cardinals—St. Louis, Missouri

13.	San Diego Padres—San Diego, California

14.	San Francisco Giants—San Francisco, California

## V.	Famous players and the legends of the game (listed here are just a few of the people that come under this category)

A.	Lou Gehrig

B.	Dave Dravecky

C.	Cy Young

D.	Christy Mathewson

E.	Frank Robinson

F.	Jimmie Foxx

G.   Babe Ruth

H.   Tom Seaver

I.   Billy Sunday

J.   Brooks Robinson

K.   Nolan Ryan

L.   Mickey Mantle

M.   Carl Yastrzemski

N.   Dale Murphy

O.   Dave Winfield

P.   Dizzy Dean

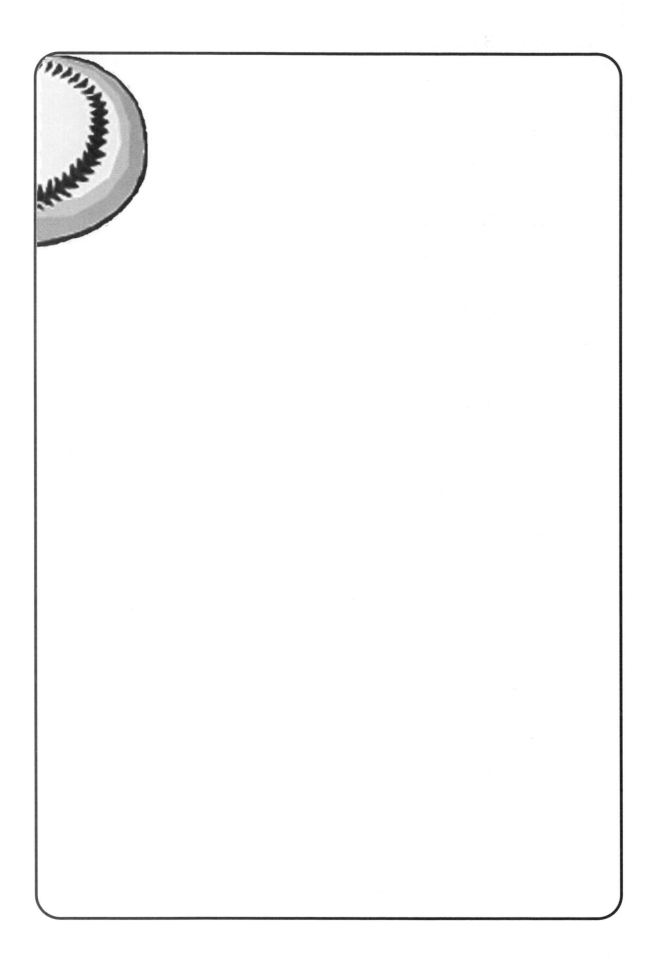

Q.   Roger Hornsby

R.   Walter Johnson

S.   Jackie Robinson

T.   Jim Abbott

U.   Rickey Henderson

V.   Roy Campanella

W.   Roberto Clemente

X.   Willie Mays

Y.   Willie Stargell

Z.   Yogi Berra

AA.   Hank Aaron

BB.   Ted Williams

CC.   Johnny Bench

DD.   Ty Cobb

EE.   Joe DiMaggio

FF.   Whitey Ford

GG.   Orel Hershiser

HH.   Reggie Jackson

II.   Sandy Koufax

JJ.   Don Mattingly

KK.   Satchel Paige

LL.   Cal Ripkin, Jr.

VI.   Baseball Awards and Recognition

A.   Most Valuable Player (MVP)

B.   Rookie of the Year

C.   Golden Glove

D.   Cy Young Award

E.   Manager of the Year

F.   National Baseball Hall of Fame

G.   League pennant

H.   World Series winner

VII.   Math in baseball

A.   Batting average (BA)

B.   Earned Run Average (ERA)

C.   Slugging Average (SLG)

D.   On-base Average (OBA)

E.   Won-Lost Percentage

F.   Standings

G.   Runs Batted In (RBIs)

VIII.   Softball—the game

A.   Developed in Chicago in 1887 as a type of indoor baseball

B.   Popular with women and girls of all ages

C.   The games usually last seven innings

D.   Ball is pitched underhand

    1.   Fast pitch

    2.   Slow pitch

E.   The field

    1.   Bases are 60 feet apart

    2.   Pitcher's mound is 46 feet from home plate

F.   The National Softball Hall of Fame and Museum

    1.   Oklahoma City, OK

    2.   Inductees include legends like Joan Joyce and Herb Dudley

IX. Baseball and softball equipment

A. Baseball

B. Softball

C. Bat

D. Gloves

E. Batting helmet

F. Uniform

G. Catcher's gear

H. Cleats and shoes

X. Baseball collectibles

A. Types of collectibles

1. Baseball cards

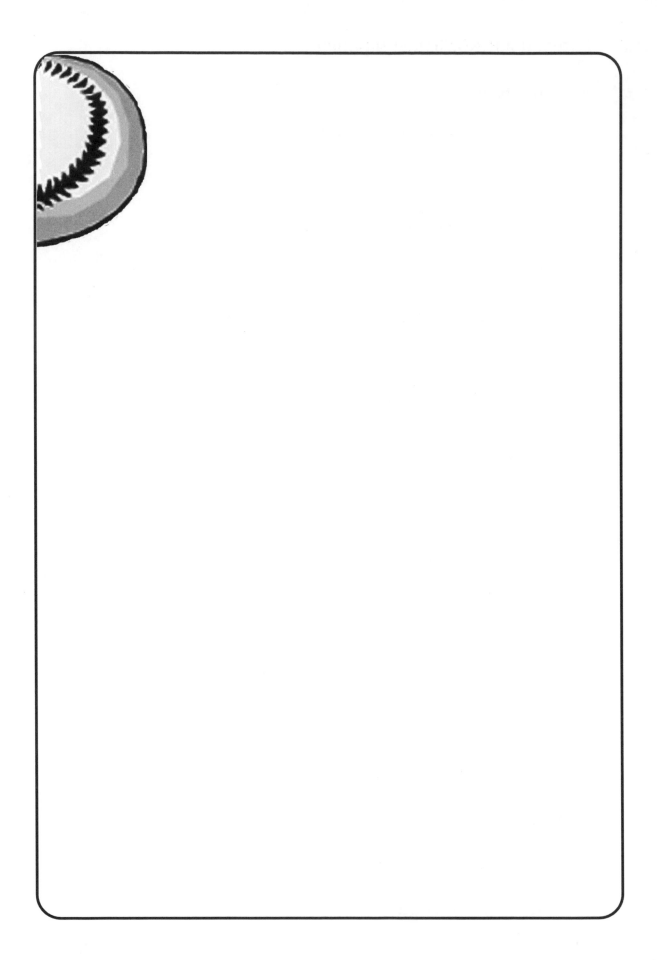

2. Baseball game ticket stubs

3. Baseball player autographs

4. Baseball art prints

5. Baseball posters

6. Baseball bats

7. Baseball caps

8. Baseball comic books

9. Baseball uniforms and shoes of players

10. Baseball team pennants

11. Letters from baseball players

B.   Enjoying a baseball collection

   1.   Purchasing the items (baseball cards seem to be the most popular collectible)

   2.   Taking care of your collection

   3.   Pricing your collectibles

   4.   Keeping track of your collection, using handwritten lists or database software on the computer

   5.   Expanding your collection through trading and buying items from others

XI.   Baseball art and music

A.   Art—there are many works of art concerning baseball for you to enjoy in this baseball Unit, and these are a few favorites

   1.   Baseball Players Practicing (1875), a watercolor painting by American master Thomas Eakins, on display at the Rhode Island School of Design

   2.   Babe Ruth (1984), a painted wooden sculpture by Armand LaMontagne, on display at the National Baseball Hall of Fame, Cooperstown, New York

3.   Baseball Game at Night (1934), an oil painting by Morris Kantor, on display at the National Museum of American Art, Smithsonian Institution, Washington, DC

4.   July Fourth (1951), an oil painting by Anna Mary Robertson Moses (Grandma Moses), on display at the White House, Washington, DC

5.   Game Called Because of Rain (1949), an illustration for the cover of the Saturday Evening Post, by Norman Rockwell, on display at the National Baseball Hall of Fame and Museum, Cooperstown, New York

6.   The Dugout (1948), an illustration for the cover of the Saturday Evening Post, by Norman Rockwell, on display at the Brooklyn Museum, Brooklyn, New York

B.   Music—there's plenty of music associated with a baseball game, and here are a few of the ones you can usually hear at a game

1.   "Take Me Out to the Ball Game", lyrics by Jack Norworth and music by Albert von Tilzer

2.   "The Star Spangled Banner" by Francis Scott Key

About The Author

Amanda Bennett, author and speaker, wife and mother of three, holds a degree in mechanical engineering. She has written this ever-growing series of unit studies for her own children, to capture their enthusiasm and nurture their gifts and talents. The concept of a thematic approach to learning is a simple one. Amanda will share this simplification through her books, allowing others to use these unit study guides to discover the amazing world that God has created for us all.

Science can be a very intimidating subject to teach, and Amanda has written this series to include science with other important areas of curriculum that apply naturally to each topic. The guides allow more time to be spent enjoying the unit study, instead of spending weeks of research time to prepare for each unit. She has shared the results of her research in the guides, including plenty of resources for areas of the study, spelling and vocabulary lists, fiction and nonfiction titles, possible careers within the topic, writing ideas, activity suggestions, addresses of manufacturers, teams, and other helpful resources.

The science-based series of guides currently includes the Unit Study Adventures titles:

Baseball	Homes
Computers	Oceans
Elections	Olympics
Electricity	Pioneers
Flight	Space
Gardens	Trains

The holiday-based series of guides currently includes the Unit Study Adventures titles:

Christmas
Thanksgiving

This planned 40-book series will soon include additional titles, which will be released periodically. We appreciate your interest. "Enjoy the Adventure."